GIFTED
&
TALEN

To develop your child's gifts and talents

MW01705289

WORD WORKBOOK

For Preschoolers

Written by Martha Cheney
Illustrated by Karol Kaminski

LOWELL HOUSE JUVENILE
LOS ANGELES
NTC/Contemporary Publishing Group

Reviewed and endorsed by Joanne López, M.A., veteran elementary educator and member of the National Association for Gifted Children.

Published by Lowell House
A division of NTC/Contemporary Publishing Group, Inc.
4255 West Touhy Avenue, Lincolnwood (Chicago), Illinois 60646-1975 U.S.A.

Copyright © 1999 by NTC/Contemporary Publishing Group, Inc.
All rights reserved. No part of this book may be reproduced, stored in a retrieval system, or transmitted in any form or by any means, electronic, mechanical, photocopying, recording, or otherwise, without the prior permission of NTC/Contemporary Publishing Group, Inc.

Managing Director and Publisher: Jack Artenstein
Director of Publishing Services: Rena Copperman
Editorial Director, Juvenile: Brenda Pope-Ostrow
Director of Art Production: Bret Perry
Educational Editor: Linda Gorman
Typesetter: Carolyn Wendt

Lowell House books can be purchased at special discounts when ordered in bulk for premiums and special sales. Please contact Customer Service at:
NTC/Contemporary Publishing Group
4255 W. Touhy Avenue
Lincolnwood, IL 60646-1975
1-800-323-4900

Printed in Hong Kong by Imago

ISBN: 1-56565-670-9

10 9 8 7 6 5 4 3 2 1

Note to Parents

GIFTED & TALENTED® WORKBOOKS will help develop your child's natural talents and gifts by providing activities to enhance critical and creative thinking skills. These skills of logic and reasoning teach children **how** to think. They are precisely the skills emphasized by teachers of gifted and talented children.

The **GIFTED & TALENTED® WORD WORKBOOK FOR PRESCHOOLERS** stimulates children's critical and creative thinking skills while expanding their vocabulary and developing their verbal skills. Fun and challenging activities introduce basic word lists for topics such as the human body, the family, animals, food, and clothes. Higher-level thinking skills promoted throughout include inference, understanding relationships, visual discrimination, and creative thinking. The top of each page is labeled to indicate the specific thinking skills developed on that page.

The **WORD WORKBOOK** also combines full-color art with black-and-white illustrations to further expand young children's learning and creativity. The full-color pages enhance preschoolers' ability to identify colors and distinguish patterns, while the black-and-white pages encourage children to use their own creative imaginations to draw or color pictures.

The activities in this workbook vary in range from easy to challenging. Read the directions to your child and explain them. Let your child choose to do the activities that interest him or her. When interest wanes, stop. A page or two at a time may be enough, as your child should have fun while learning.

GIFTED & TALENTED® WORKBOOKS have been written and endorsed by educators. These books will benefit any child who demonstrates curiosity, imagination, a sense of fun and wonder about the world, and a desire to learn. They will open your child's mind to new experiences and help fulfill his or her true potential.

LET'S DANCE!

Name each body part you see in the picture. Find that same part of your own body and give it a shake or a wiggle!
Where is your elbow? Where is your ankle?
What do you have at the end of each hand?
How many toes do you have?
What joins your head to your shoulders?

Now it's your turn to try the dance that the children are doing. Do these movements in order:

Shake your arms and legs.
Stamp your feet.
Nod your head.
Clap your hands.
Wiggle your fingers and toes.

Get your whole family to join in!

JUST LIKE YOU!

What do you look like? Finish this picture to make it look like you. Color the eyes and skin to match yours. Add some hair that looks like yours. Write your name under the picture.

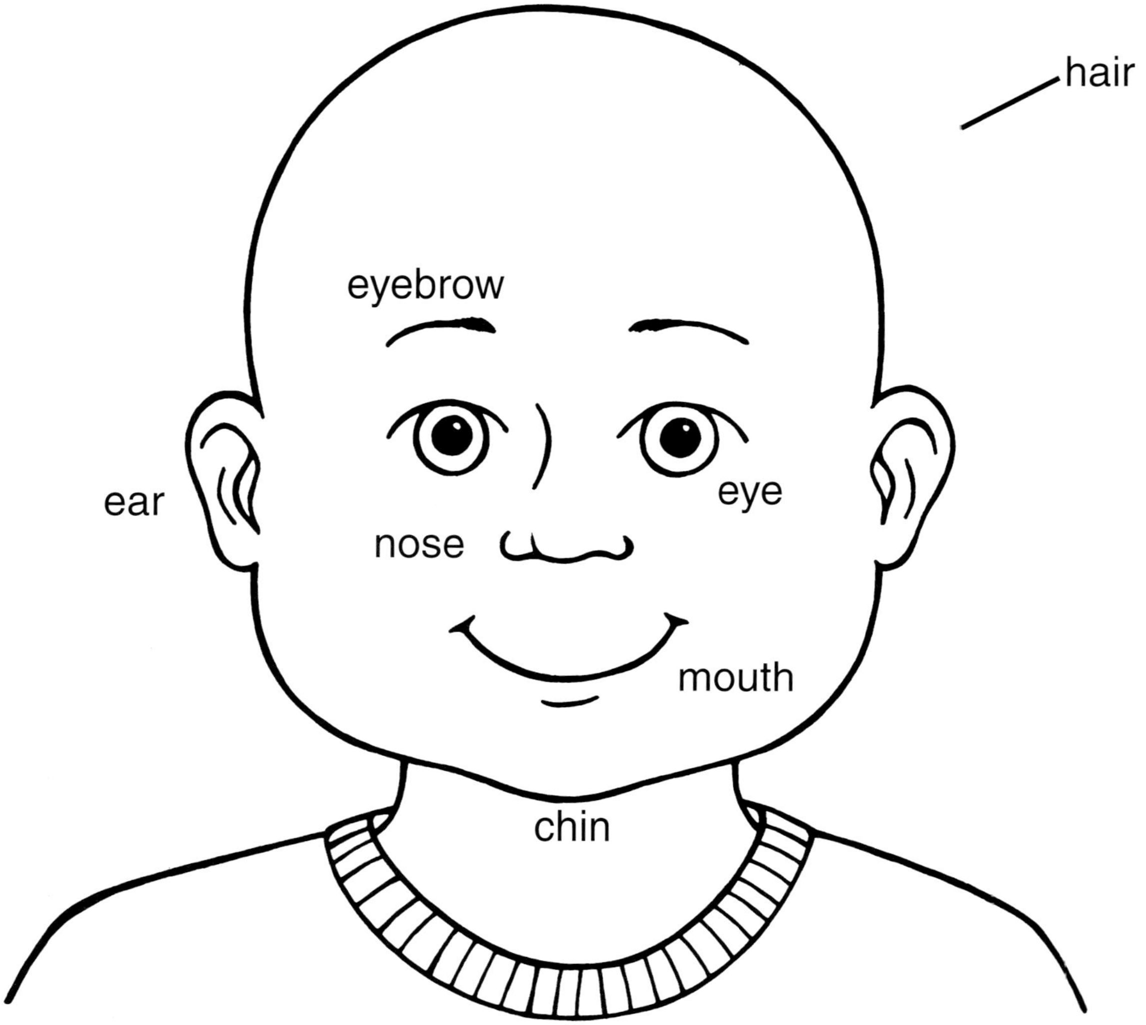

____

(your name)

What do your eyes do?
What do your ears do?

FAMILY TIME

This is a family.
Who is the biggest member of the family? Color his or her clothes blue.
Who is the smallest member of the family? Color his or her clothes red.

The family tried to line up from biggest to smallest, but one of them is out of order! Which member of the family is not in the right place? Where should that person be?

FAMILY VISIT

Families come in all shapes and sizes.
Here are some of the people who might be a part of your family.
Can you name them all?

What is the grandmother doing?
Who is sleeping?
Which member of the family is the youngest?
Who is just arriving?
Is the family happy to be together? How do you know?

HOME, SWEET HOME

Here are two different kinds of homes for people.
What is on top of the house? Color it brown.
What do you have to open to get into the apartment building?
Color them green.

What comes out of the chimney?
Which home has more steps?
Which one of these homes is more like yours?

A COZY BEDROOM

Here is a cozy bedroom for you to color.
Color the object that you rest your head on purple.
Color the object that gives off light yellow.
Color the rest of the picture any way you like.

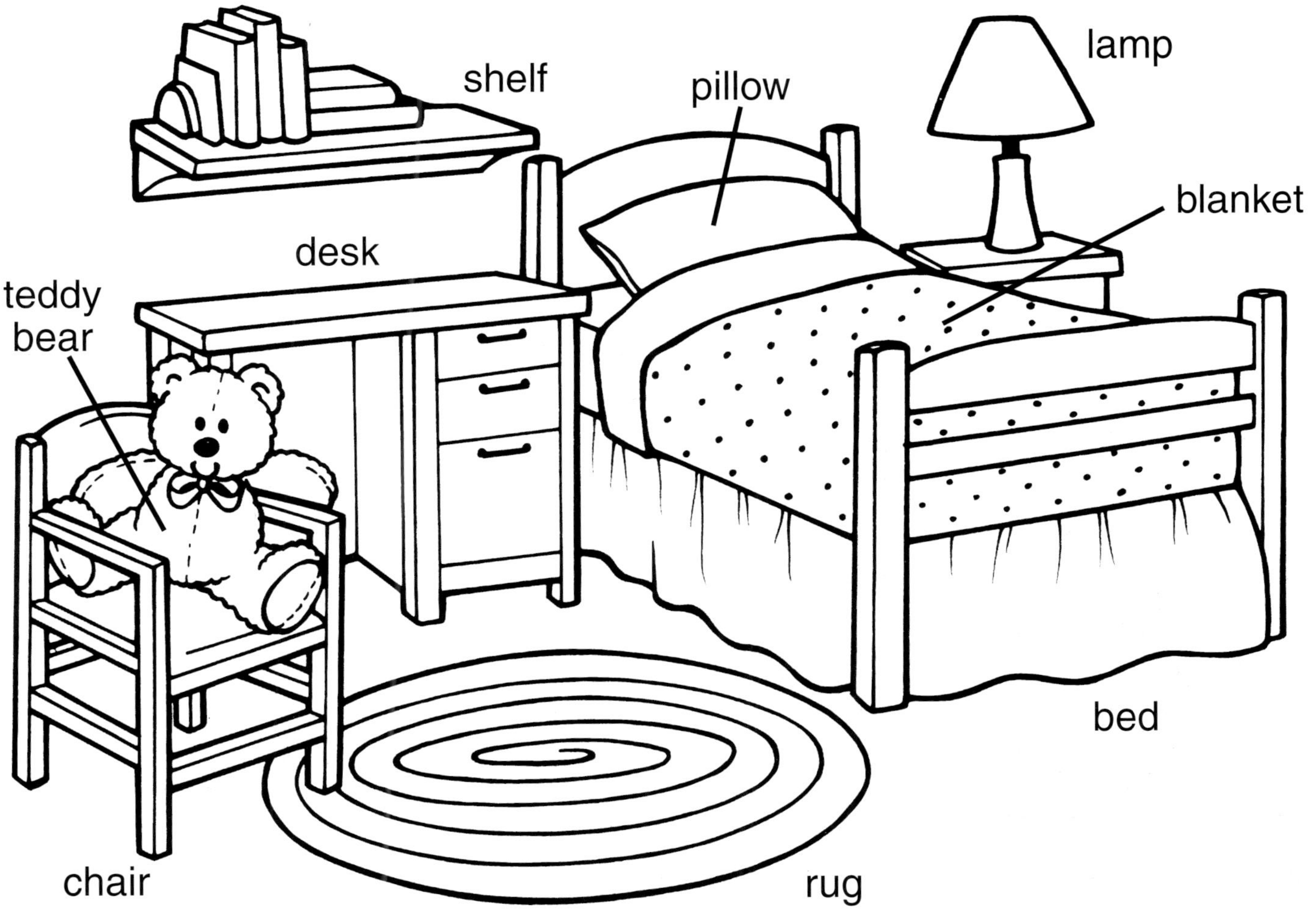

What do you see on the floor?
What is sitting in the chair?
On a separate sheet of paper, draw a picture of your own bedroom. What things in your drawing are in this picture?

SPRING SHOWERS

These children are playing outside on a rainy spring afternoon.
What is the girl doing?
What is the boy doing?
What clothes help the children stay dry?
What is the colorful object in the sky?

Do you think the children like the rain? Why?

SUMMER SUNSHINE

A hot summer day is the perfect time to go to the beach. What are some fun things to do there?

What are the children looking at?
What do you think might be in the basket?

FRISKY FALL FUN

Fall brings cool weather and colorful leaves. What colors should the leaves in this picture be? Color the leaves to show that it is fall.

Look at the clothes that the children are wearing.

Color the jeans blue.

Color the cowboy boots red.

Color the rest of the picture any way you like.

What are the children doing? Which one is working? Which one is playing?

WINTER WONDERLAND

There are lots of fun things to do in the wintertime. But it is cold outside, so everyone needs to wear warm clothes. What are the children wearing on their feet? Color one pair red and one pair blue.
What is the boy wearing on his hands? Color them yellow.
What is the snowman wearing around its neck? Color it green.

What winter sport is the girl going to do?
Why doesn't the snowman need a coat?

IN THE FOREST

Many different kinds of wild animals live in the forest. Find some animals that are big. Find some animals that are small.
Which animal has stripes?
What is the wolf doing?

Which animals have antlers on their heads?
Which animal can fly?
How many tails do you see?
How many animals do you see altogether?
Why do you think some of the animals are hiding?

AT THE FARM

Let's go visit the animals at the farm!
Which animals are near the barn?
Where is the rooster? Color it red.
Which animals are following the hen? Color them yellow.
Color the rest of the picture any way you like.

Where is the cat? What is it doing?
Which animals are in the pen? What sound do they make?
Which animal gives milk? What sound does it make?
Which animals would make good pets? Why?

ZOO ANIMALS

At the zoo, you can see wild animals that come from all over the world.

Find the animals that have stripes. What are they?

Where is the monkey? What food does it like to eat?

Which animal can hop?

Which animal is next to the tiger?

Find an animal that has spots. Why do you think it has a long neck?

Which animals like the water?

Find the animal with the biggest ears. What color is it?

Which animal is black?

How many animals do you see altogether?

Which is your favorite zoo animal? Why?

BY THE POND

Here are some of the animals that live at the pond.
Which animal is on the log? Color it brown.
Which animal has a shell? Color it green.
Which animals live underwater? Color them yellow.

Which objects in the picture can float?
Which animals can fly?
Why do you think the girl likes to come to the pond?

YOUR FAVORITE ANIMAL

Draw a picture of your favorite animal. Ask an adult to help you write the name of the animal on the line.

MY FAVORITE ANIMAL

____

Does your favorite animal have fur?
How many legs does it have?
What does it like to eat?

FUN AT THE PARK

These children are having fun at the park.
What are the children doing?
Which children are near the ground?
Which children are in the air?

Find the child who is inside the playhouse.
What else in the picture is inside something?
Find the child who is crawling under the ribbon.
What else in the picture is under something?
What things do you like to do at the park?

BIG MOUSE, LITTLE MOUSE

Finish the picture of the mice using the clues.

The big mouse is happy.
The little mouse is sad.
The big mouse has little ears.
The little mouse has big ears.
The big mouse has a long tail.
The little mouse has a short tail.

Why do you think the little mouse is sad?

LET'S HAVE LUNCH!

These children are having lunch together.
Can you find something in the picture that is hot? Can you find something that is cold?
Which glass is empty? Which glass is full?

What has just happened? What should the boy do next?

FRUIT AND FLOWERS

Fred has lots of fruit and flowers for sale. Everything he sells is red or purple.

What red fruits are for sale?

What purple fruits are for sale?

What kind of red flowers do you see?

What kind of purple flowers do you see?

Can you find some things in your home that are red?

Can you find some things in your home that are purple?

TROPICAL TREATS

Tina is having a wonderful vacation on a tropical island.
What yellow things can Tina eat?
What orange things can Tina eat?
Can you find something that is yellow and hot?
Can you find something that is orange and can fly?

Why do you think Tina is wearing a hat?

A FRIENDLY CATERPILLAR

Gordon is having a picnic lunch in his favorite park.
Find the green objects in the picture using the clues. Color each object green.

It is something to eat.
It is a furry little insect.
They grow on a tree.
It grows on the ground.

Color the rest of the picture any way you like.

Tell a story about what is happening in the picture.

BETTY BLUE

Betty Blue likes to juggle. She only juggles things that are blue. Color each object that Betty is juggling blue.
Which object can bounce?
Which object makes a pretty sound?
Which object could you find in a library?
Which object could you use to pack things in?

What letter of the alphabet do all the blue objects begin with?

A PERFECT PAIR

Look at all the rabbits! Only two rabbits look exactly alike.
Can you find them?
What color is their fur?
Do these rabbits have patches? What color are they?
What color are their noses?

RAINBOW BIRD

Look at the beautiful bird! Can you name all the colors you see on the bird?

What is the bird's mouth called?

What does the bird use to fly?

What does the bird use to hold on to the branch?

If you could fly, where would you go?

A SHAPE CASTLE

Here are four different shapes. Can you say the name of each shape?

Look at the shape castle.
How many squares do you see?
How many circles do you see?
How many rectangles do you see?
How many triangles do you see?
Color the castle any way you like.

Who lives in a castle? Make up a story about something that could happen in a magic castle.

HIDDEN SHAPES

Here are four different shapes. Can you say the name of each shape?

heart diamond crescent oval

These shapes are hidden in the picture below.
Can you find 4 hearts? Can you find 3 crescents?
Can you find 4 diamonds? Can you find 3 ovals?

Can you find any of these shapes in the kitchen of your home?

NUMBER WORDS

Count the number of objects in each box on this page and the next page.
How many candy canes are there?
How many ladybugs are there?
Are there more stars than buttons?
Which object is there the most of?
Which object is there the fewest of?

1 one snowflake

2 two cupcakes

3 three lollipops

4 four candy canes

5 five stars

6 six ladybugs

7 seven feathers

8 eight buttons

9 nine crayons

10 ten jelly beans

A BACKYARD BIRTHDAY PARTY

The children are having a birthday party. Look at all the yummy food to eat!
Which foods taste good hot?
Which foods taste good cold?
Which food do you like best?

Whose birthday is it? How do you know?
What clue tells you how old this child is?
What do you think the present could be?

AT THE SUPERMARKET

Ryan and Monica are shopping at the supermarket.
What foods do you see in their basket?
What do you think they're planning to make?

Find some foods you could use to make breakfast.
Find some foods you could use to make lunch.
What could you buy if you were thirsty?
Which foods do you have to cook before you eat them?

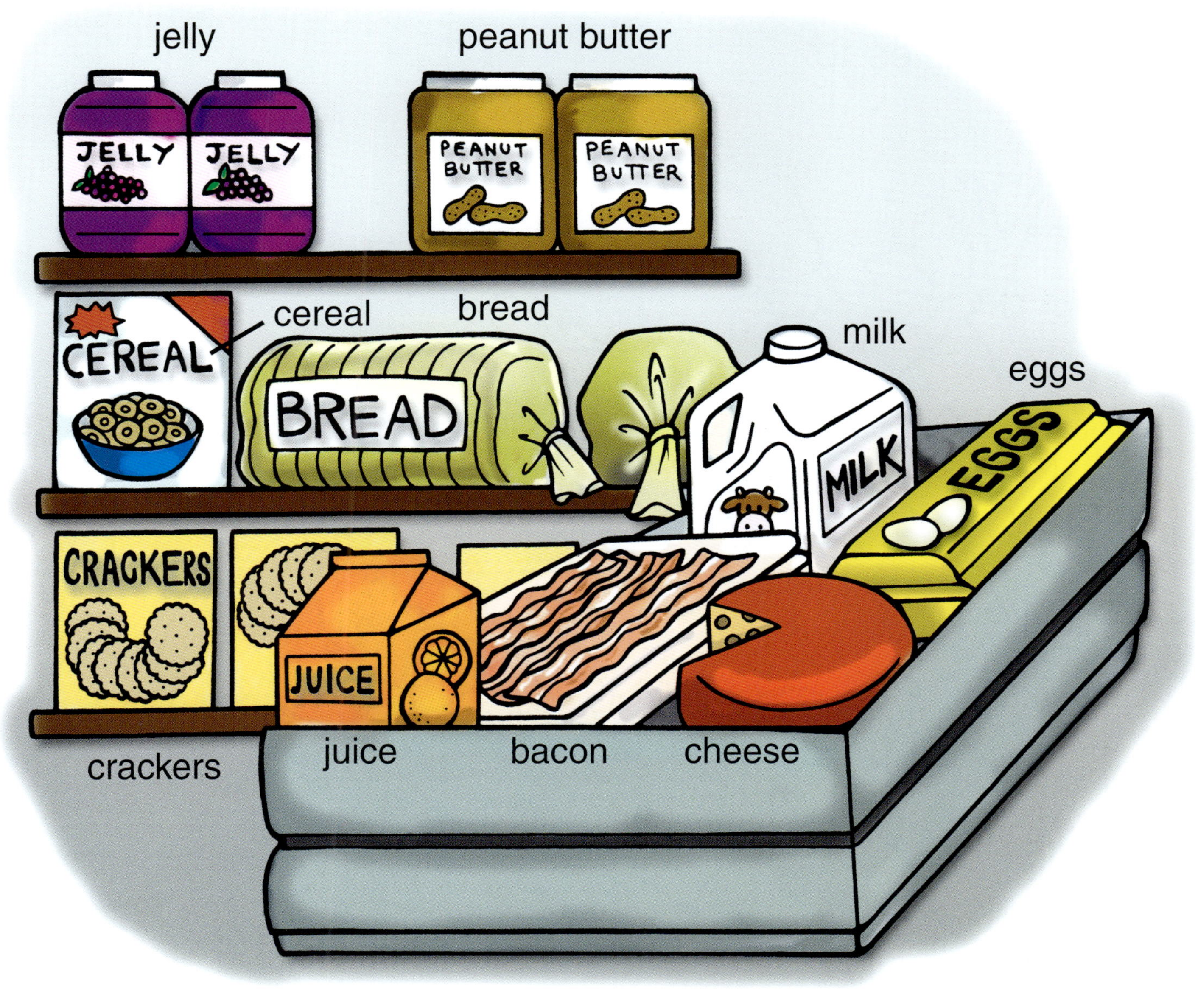

ACTION WORDS

Can you finish each sentence below and on the next page? Ask an adult to help you. Look at the pictures for clues.

The girl likes to ________________.

The baby likes to ________________.

The father likes to ________________.

The squirrel likes to ________________.

The big dog likes to ________________.
The little dog likes to ________________.
The cat likes to ________________.
The police officer likes to ________________.

BOATS AFLOAT

There are lots of different kinds of boats. Do you know what kinds of boats these are?
Which boats are moved by people rowing or paddling?
Which boat is moved by the wind?
Which boat can go across the ocean?

What kind of bird lives near the water? Can you find it in the picture?
What is the biggest animal in the picture?
What animal is jumping out of the water?
What is the dog sitting on?
What are the children wearing for safety?

MOVIN' ON

A vehicle is something you can ride in or on. Here are some different kinds of vehicles.

Which vehicles carry only one person?

Which vehicles can carry more than one person?

What is the boy wearing for safety?

Do all the vehicles have wheels?

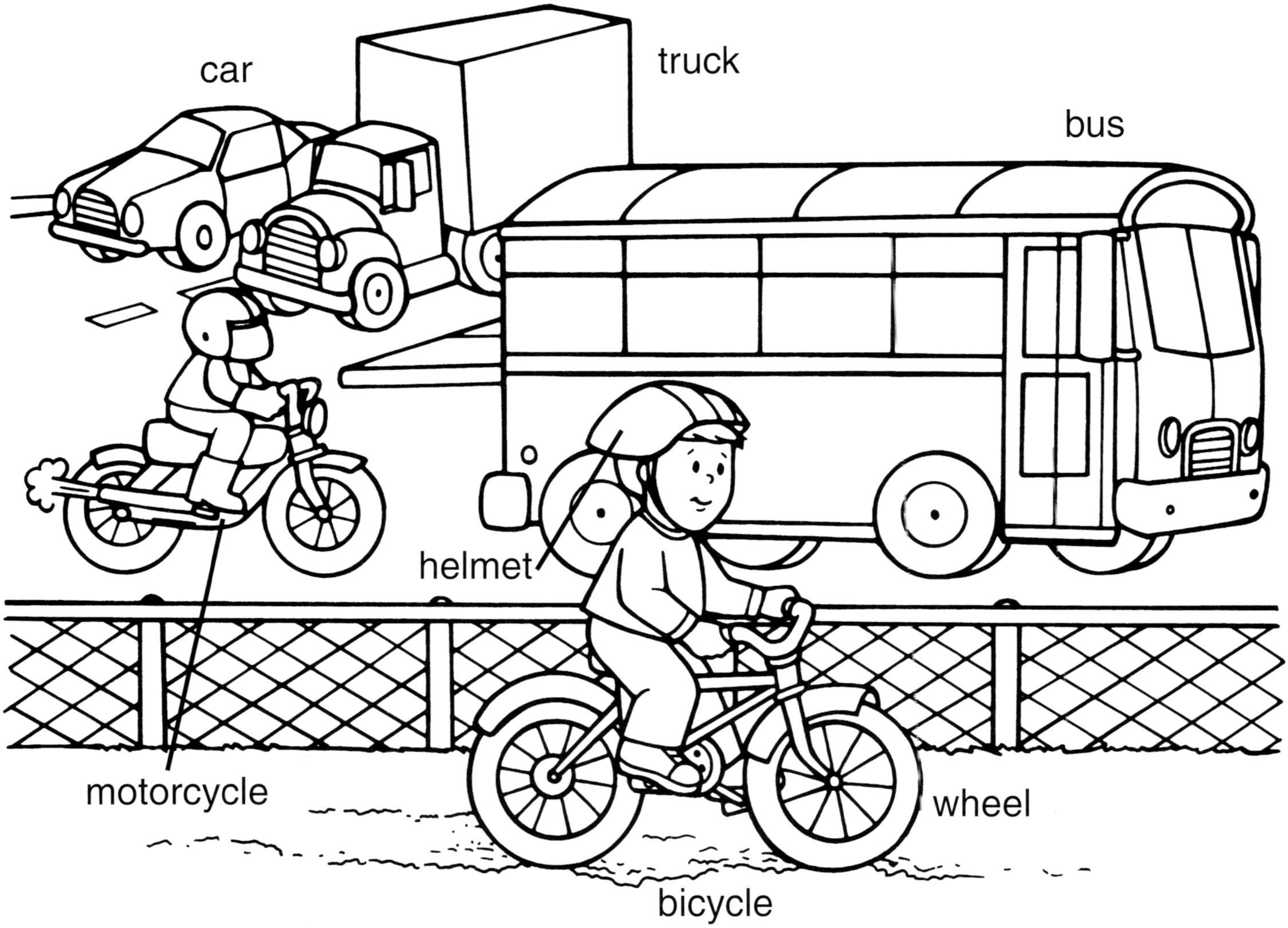

Where do you think the boy might be going?

ACROSS THE MOUNTAINS

Here are some other kinds of vehicles that people can ride in.
Which vehicles can fly?
Which vehicle is on the track?
Which vehicle do you think can move the fastest?

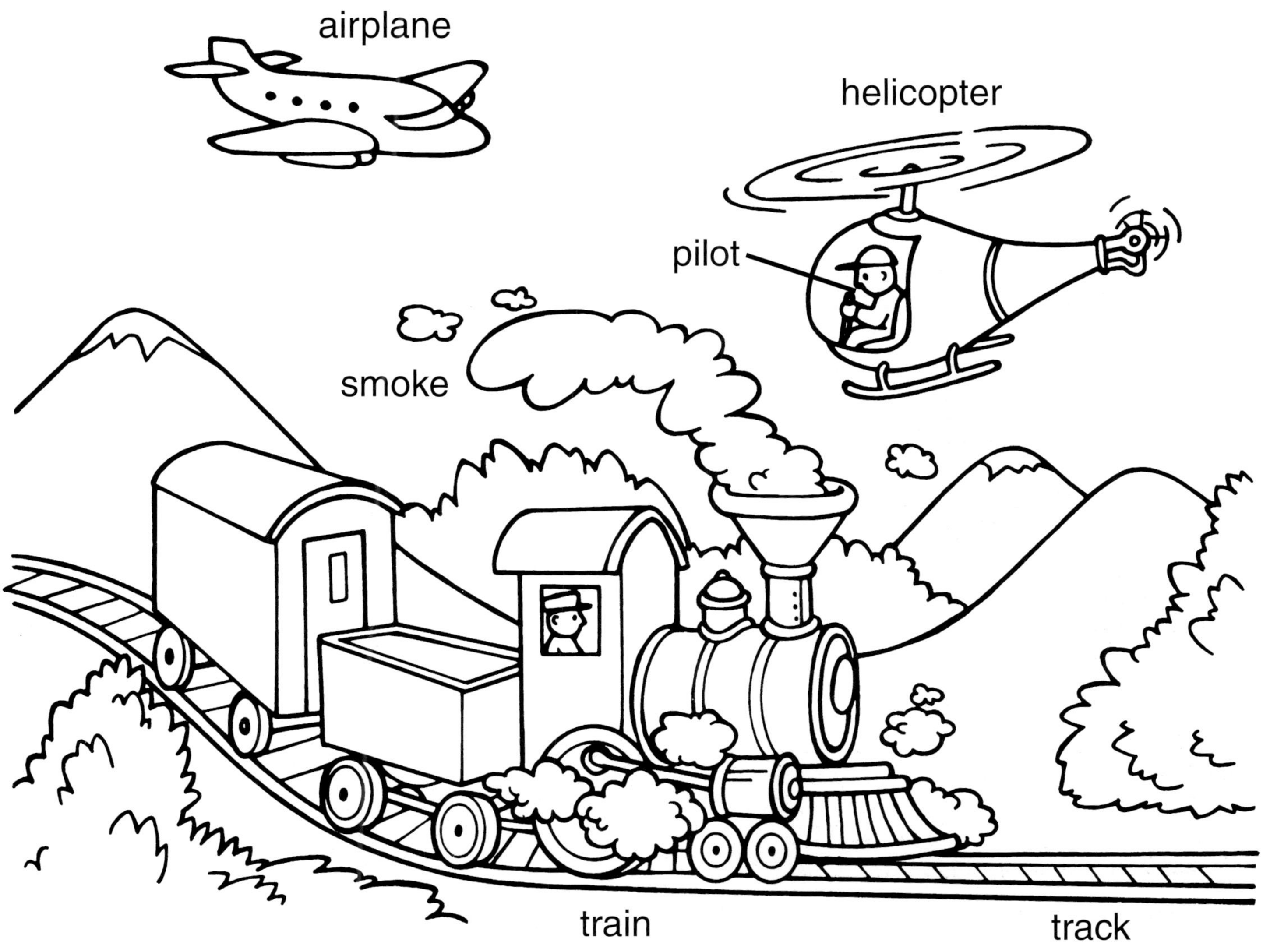

What is your favorite vehicle?
If you could go anywhere, where would you go?

LET'S CELEBRATE!

____

(your name)

Is Wonderful with Words!